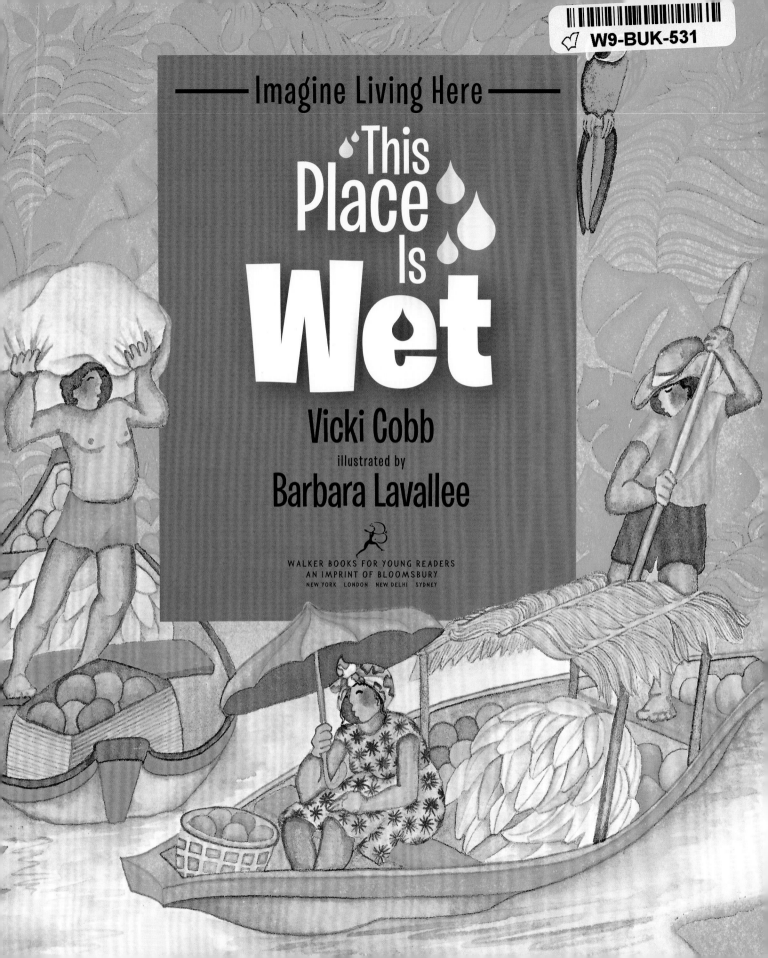

Imagine Living Here

This Place Is Wet

Vicki Cobb

illustrated by

Barbara Lavallee

WALKER BOOKS FOR YOUNG READERS
AN IMPRINT OF BLOOMSBURY
NEW YORK   LONDON   NEW DELHI   SYDNEY

The author and artist gratefully acknowledge the support and assistance
of the following: Eliane Freitas of the Brazilian Tourism Foundation;
Scott A. Mori, curator of the New York Botanical Gardens; Paolo Lavageto
of Varig Brazilian Airlines; Ivano Freitas Cordiero, Claudia Simoes, and Huberto
Cetraro of Emamtur in Manaus; Bruce Nelson and Francisco Colares of INPA;
2nd Sgt. Carlos Alberto Lima, Eury and Tralcy Barros, and Alionar Barros of
Amazon Explorers; Dr. Francisco Ritta Bernardino of the Ariau Tower Lodge;
Ivandel Godhino of Embratur; and, more recently, Dr. Richard Reed of Trinity
University for double-checking the information about jaguar hunting.

Original text copyright © 1989 by Vicki Cobb
Updated text copyright © 2013 by Vicki Cobb
Illustrations copyright © 1989 by Barbara Lavallee

First published in the United States of America in 1989; revised edition published in May 2013
by Walker Books for Young Readers, an imprint of Bloomsbury Publishing, Inc.
www.bloomsbury.com

For information about permission to reproduce selections from this book, write to
Permissions, Walker BFYR, 175 Fifth Avenue, New York, New York 10010
Bloomsbury books may be purchased for business or promotional use. For information on bulk purchases please contact
Macmillan Corporate and Premium Sales Department at specialmarkets@macmillan.com

The Library of Congress has cataloged the original edition as follows:
Cobb, Vicki.
This place is wet / by Vicki Cobb ; illustrated by Barbara Lavallee.
p.   cm.—(Imagine living here)
Summary: Focuses on the land, ecology, people, and animals of the Amazon rain forest in Brazil, presenting it
as an example of a place where there is so much water that some houses need to be built on stilts.
ISBN 0-8027-8880-6 (hardcover) • ISBN 0-8027-6881-4 (reinforced)
ISBN 0-8027-7399-0 (paperback)
1. Rain forest ecology—Amazon River Region—Juvenile literature. 2. Rain forest ecology—Brazil—Juvenile literature.
3. Amazon River Region—Description and travel—Juvenile literature. 4. Brazil—Description and travel—Juvenile literature.
[1. Rain forest ecology—Amazon River Region. 2. Amazon River Region—Description and travel. 3. Brazil—Description and travel.]
I. Lavallee, Barbara, ill. II. Title. III. Series: Cobb, Vicki. Imagine living here.
QH112.C63 1989   574.5'2642'09811—dc20   89-32445   CIP   AC

ISBN 978-0-8027-3400-6 (revised)

Art created with transparent watercolor painted on 300 lb Fabriano cold pressed watercolor paper
Typeset in Amasis Std
Book design by Regina Roff

Printed in China by C&C Offset Printing Co., Ltd., Shenzhen, Guangdong
1 3 5 7 9 10 8 6 4 2

💧 Hot and Humid! 💧

The minute you step out of your airplane in Manaus, Brazil, your skin quickly becomes coated with a thin film of moisture. Your clothes stick to you. You feel as if you have stepped inside a tropical hothouse. In fact, you *are* in a natural hothouse, an overgrown place called a tropical rain forest. The equatorial sun shines on puddles left by a recent shower that didn't cool things off. Air-conditioning condenses moisture on windows, and carpeted rooms smell of mildew. The yearly rainfall here is about 97 inches (246 centimeters), more than 8 feet (2.4 meters), and the average humidity is 85 percent. No doubt about it; this place is wet!

A City on the World's Biggest River

Manaus is a city of more than one and a half million people in the heart of the rain forest in northern Brazil, just south of the equator. The city is on the banks of the Rio Negro, the "black river." It is named for its strong-tea color, which comes from rotting plants. The Rio Negro flows into the most enormous river in the world, the Amazon, which begins at a spring-fed lake high in the Andes Mountains of southern Peru, and continues east across South America for 4,195 miles (6,751 kilometers), where it empties into the Atlantic Ocean.

More than one thousand streams and rivers join the Amazon on its way to the sea. Together, they hold more water than the next eight largest rivers combined, making the Amazon the largest in the world when measured by volume. But scientists now believe that it is also the longest river, beating the Nile by 65 miles (104.6 km).

Floods Are Normal

The streams and rivers of the Amazon basin do not always stay in their banks. Flooding is normal six months out of the year. The high water mark in July can be 40 to 60 feet (12 to 18 m) higher than the low mark in December. Forests and fields are flooded, islands and beaches disappear, and there are many new waterways among the trees. Houses on the waterfront float or are built on stilts. During the wet season, the Amazon near Manaus may be 35 miles (56 km) wide, while only 7 miles (11 km) wide during the dry season.

💧 Plants Love It Here 💧

Lots of water and warm weather are the best possible conditions for plant growth, and the rain forest is living proof. A typical tree is 100 to 130 feet (30.5 to 39.6 m) tall, with shallow roots, a thin bare trunk, and a small crown of leaves at the top. Its crown is right next to the crowns of other trees. Together, the treetops form the roof of the forest, which is called the "canopy layer."

Rain-forest trees and plants compete for the sunlight they need to stay alive. The only chance for a new tree to grow is when an old tree falls, creating a gap filled with sunlight. Some plants, like orchids, grow in the branches of trees. They are called *epiphytes* (EP-eh-fites). Epiphyte roots never touch the ground but hang in the air, absorbing moisture. There are also vines that climb trees to reach the sun.

The forest canopy is so thick that the forest floor is in deep shade. But there are plants there too, ones well-suited to dim light. Most houseplants come from the rain-forest floor.

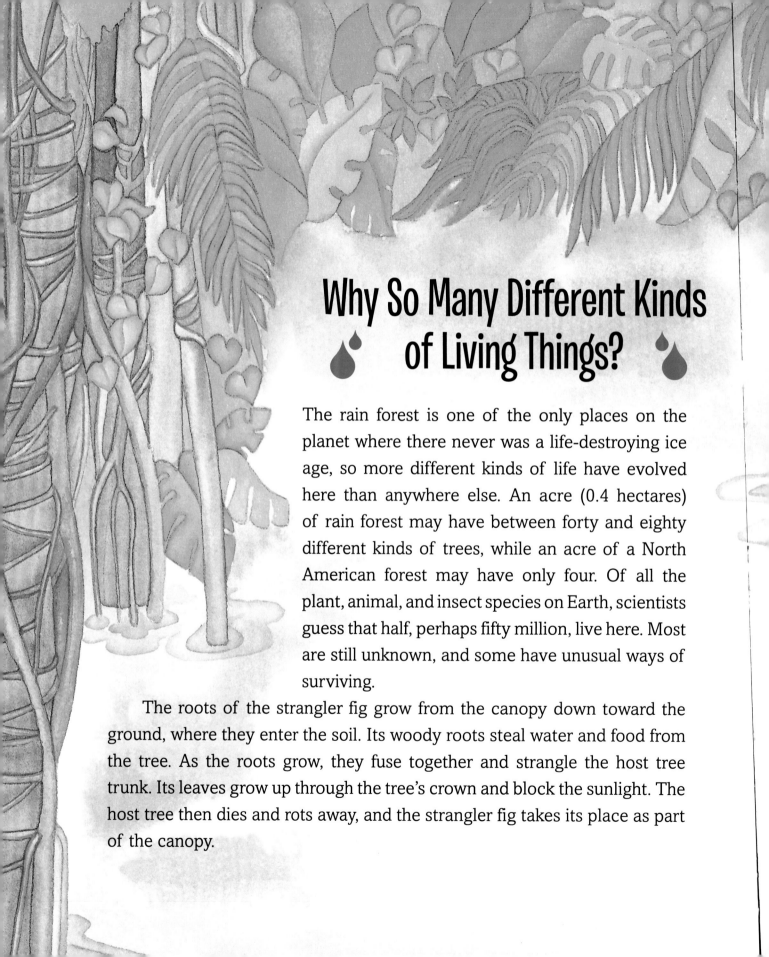

Why So Many Different Kinds of Living Things?

The rain forest is one of the only places on the planet where there never was a life-destroying ice age, so more different kinds of life have evolved here than anywhere else. An acre (0.4 hectares) of rain forest may have between forty and eighty different kinds of trees, while an acre of a North American forest may have only four. Of all the plant, animal, and insect species on Earth, scientists guess that half, perhaps fifty million, live here. Most are still unknown, and some have unusual ways of surviving.

The roots of the strangler fig grow from the canopy down toward the ground, where they enter the soil. Its woody roots steal water and food from the tree. As the roots grow, they fuse together and strangle the host tree trunk. Its leaves grow up through the tree's crown and block the sunlight. The host tree then dies and rots away, and the strangler fig takes its place as part of the canopy.

The shallow roots of rain-forest trees are not a good anchor in strong winds or floods. Vines and closeness to other trees help to keep them from blowing over. Some trees, like the giant kapok, have flat buttresses around the bottom of the trunk for added support. These buttresses make a booming sound, like a drum, when hit. Rain-forest Indians communicate through the forest by striking them.

Unusual Partnerships

Some plants and animals work in partnerships to survive. The flower of the Brazil-nut tree is pollinated by a bee shaped to fit exactly inside the flower, like a piece of a jigsaw puzzle. When the woody fruit of the tree drops to the ground, an agouti, a ratlike animal, gnaws it open and carries away the nuts to bury them for future use. This way, the seeds are spread through the forest. Forgotten seeds may someday become trees.

Wild Brazil-nut trees grow here and there among other rain-forest trees. People tried planting a Brazil-nut plantation for easier harvesting. The trees grew very well but they never bore fruit. Why? There were no bees to pollinate the flowers. It seems that the bees need more than Brazil-nut flowers in order to live. But scientists could not figure out what that was. Living things depend on each other in mysterious ways. Break a chain and a species can perish.

The lily pads of the Victoria royal water lily, which grow in shallow backwaters, can be 8 feet (2.4 m) across. Underneath, the heavy ribs of its leaves have spines to protect it from plant-eating fish. When its large white flower opens at sunset, its ripe pineapple smell and surface warmth—as much as 9 degrees Fahrenheit (5.5 degrees Celsius) warmer than the air—immediately draw large brown beetles. They feed in the center of the flower. A few hours later, the flower closes, trapping the beetles until the following evening when the flower opens again. But now the flower is cool, no longer smells, and is a deep red or purple color. The beetles crawl out, covered with pollen, which they deliver to the next white flower they visit that evening. The beetle gets its meal, and the royal water lily gets pollinated.

Rain-Forest Giants

The Amazon has animals that match the strangeness of the plants that grow there. The largest snake in the world is the anaconda. A full-grown anaconda is at least 30 feet (9.1 m) long and weighs up to 600 pounds (272 kilograms). The Amazon caiman alligator can be 15 feet (4.6 m) long. In the night their eyes glow like red coals when you shine a bright light on them. The electric eel of the Amazon gives off enough of a shock to stun a person unconscious. The largest beetle is the Hercules, which is 7 inches (17.8 cm) long. The largest rat is the capybara. It may grow to be 4 feet (1.2 m) long and weigh 100 pounds (45.4 kg) or more. The electric-blue morpho butterfly has a wingspan up to 7 inches (17.8 cm) across. It's not the largest in the world but its wingspan is larger than that of many birds.

The tambaqui (tam-bah-KEE), also known as the "fat fish," can be 3 feet (0.9 m) long and weigh 60 pounds (27.2 kg). Its mouthful of teeth is perfect for cracking both nuts and its favorite food, rubber-tree seeds, which it turns into body fat. Broiled tambaqui tastes more like lamb than fish.

Tambaqui is a cousin of the fearsome 15-inch (38-cm) piranha. Piranhas feed by taking bites out of other fish and animals with their razor-sharp triangular teeth. A school of piranhas has been known to devour a cow in a few minutes, each fish taking only a few bites. In spite of the many stories about ferocious piranhas, they don't often attack people.

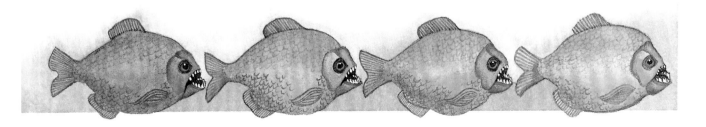

Endangered Mammals

Unfortunately, the remarkable Amazon river mammals have attracted hunters and trappers who have hunted them almost to extinction. The largest otter in the world lives here. This playful fishing champion can be more than 6 feet (1.8 m) long. Its fur is particularly beautiful. Pink and gray freshwater dolphins leap out of the water at one of their favorite feeding areas: where the black water of the Rio Negro meets the muddy waters

of the Amazon. The two rivers flow side by side without mixing for about 10 miles (16 km), until the muddy waters take over and give the Amazon the color of coffee with milk.

Manatees, or sea cows, graze on floating plants of the Amazon. They have been hunted for their meat and skin, which makes soft leather. All of the river mammals are now protected by law.

Animals in the Canopy

Some animals of the rain forest live up in the canopy and almost never touch the ground their whole lives. The slow-moving sloth spends its life upside down, hanging from trees with its hook-shaped claws. Its fur grows from its belly toward its back so rainwater can run off easily in its upside-down position.

Microscopic green plants grow in its fur, giving the sloth a protective green color.

Monkeys are the forest acrobats. The spider monkey's tail is twice as long as its body. It works like a fifth hand as the monkey swings through the treetops. At sunrise and sunset the loud roars of the howler monkeys sound like thunder. Howler bands of about twenty monkeys make noise to warn other bands of monkeys to stay away from where they're feeding.

Even louder than the howler monkeys are the parrots. Their hoarse squawks fill the air at the end of the day as they fly in pairs to nest for the night. Parrot beaks are nutcrackers, strong enough to crack open Brazil nuts. At night, the forest canopy is also noisy with the sound of bat wings. Many different trees depend on bats for pollination. The drab flowers have odors similar to sweat or meat to attract bats. There are also many fruit-eating bats that spread seeds in the canopy.

Danger on the Ground

One of the most dangerous animals of the jungle is the jaguar. A full-grown jaguar will hunt and eat an animal the size of a capybara a week. It can easily climb trees and will swim after an alligator. In the past, some Indian tribes considered killing a jaguar to be the work of a grown man and that this signaled a boy's arrival at manhood. They did not use guns, but wooden spears or bows and arrows.

Other young people continue to prove their bravery by putting a hand into a straw mitt filled with tiny, venomous fire ants and letting the stinging ants bite away. If the elder judges think these twelve- or thirteen-year-old boys or girls aren't brave enough, they get another chance the next year. Fire-ant bites are painful and some people have a delayed reaction weeks later, ranging from a bad itch to a fever and occasionally even death.

Wealth from the Forest

In spite of all the dangers of the Brazilian rain forest, people from all over the world have settled here. Manaus was first settled as a small Portuguese fort in 1669, and for many years it was just a sleepy jungle town.

The invention of the rubber automobile tire at the end of the nineteenth century changed everything. The rubber trees in the rain forest bleed a sticky white sap called *latex* when the trunk is cut. Latex can be collected and processed to form straw-colored balls of raw rubber. Rubber brought thousands of people to Manaus. Some people made fortunes and built the city into a showplace of fancy houses and theaters.

But the boom lasted only twenty-five years. Rubber-tree seeds were smuggled to plantations in Malaysia. It was easier to collect latex from neat rows of trees than from wild trees growing here and there in the jungle. People no longer needed expensive rubber from Brazil. Manaus again became a quiet city.

Destroying the Rain Forest

Some settlers became farmers. They needed to clear away the trees in order to create fields and pastures. Since there were no roads to drag chopped-down trees away to sawmills, the fallen trees were burned. This kind of land clearing is called "slash and burn." The main farm crop is manioc, a starchy root that can be made into a cake or a pancake. It can also be made into a dry yellowish sandy powder, called tapioca, which is sprinkled on foods like salt.

People thought that clearing the rain forest would produce rich farmland for many different kinds of crops. They were wrong. Rain-forest soil is poor. Rotting leaves from the trees become a natural fertilizer, but when the trees are cut down, this source of fertilizer is gone. The rains wash the minerals out of the exposed soil, and it is too expensive to add fertilizer and minerals after the soil gives out. So the land is abandoned. Farmers move on and slash and burn new areas of the forest.

Small cleared areas can become a part of the forest again, but large cleared areas don't recover.

Today there is a monster machine that can clear a path in the rain forest 4 miles (6.4 km) long and 26 feet (7.9 m) wide in an hour. Its boom easily knocks over the trees, and knife-bladed rollers chop them up as it moves along.

The Trans-Amazon Highway, which was bulldozed through the jungle in the early 1970s, was supposed to open up the wilderness to new settlers, but it has been a huge failure. With the trees removed, there was nothing to hold the soil during the heavy rains. Unpaved roadways washed away. Even under paved sections, soil washed away. Although there are sections of paved roads, easy highway travel for long distances is still impossible. Trucks stuck up to their hubcaps in the red mud are a common sight during the rainy season.

The rain forest is also being destroyed for its valuable hardwood trees, such as mahogany, and to get at gold, iron, and other riches in its earth. Gold was discovered deep in the jungle in 1980 when a tree blew over and chunks of gold were found in the dirt around its roots.

This discovery created a gold rush. The Brazilian government gave tens of thousands of poor Brazilian workers claims that

were 6 feet by 9 feet (1.8 m by 2.7 m). Sifted dirt was carried out because there was no room for it in the mine. The mine was closed in 1986 after a landslide caused many deaths. Today that open pit is a polluted lake, and there will be a new mine on the site in 2013.

People have to find a balance between the loss of the wilderness and the needs of the villages and cities.

Power and Pollution

A hydroelectric plant near Manaus uses river water to make electricity. Since the Amazon doesn't flow fast enough to turn the turbines, the Balbina Dam was built to create a huge lake. Water falling from the lake generates electricity, but the lake flooded and destroyed thousands of acres (hectares) of rain forest.

The rising waters trapped many animals. Two hundred and fifty men went out in canoes every day for a year to rescue the animals, but many

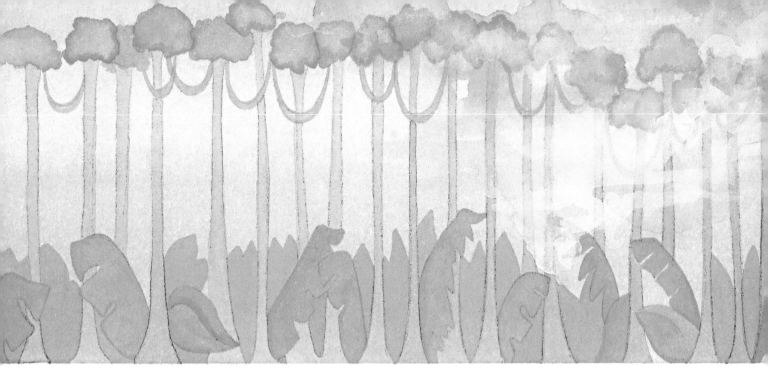

drowned. The plants and animals covered by the lake rot, and gases, like carbon dioxide, bubble to the surface, where they escape into the air and add to the problem of air pollution.

The biggest destroyer of the rain forest is still man-made fires. On some days in the dry season, there are thousands of fires burning across the Amazon basin to clear the land. Plants and animals that have not yet been discovered are destroyed. More important, the fires are adding to the world's air pollution problem by producing carbon dioxide.

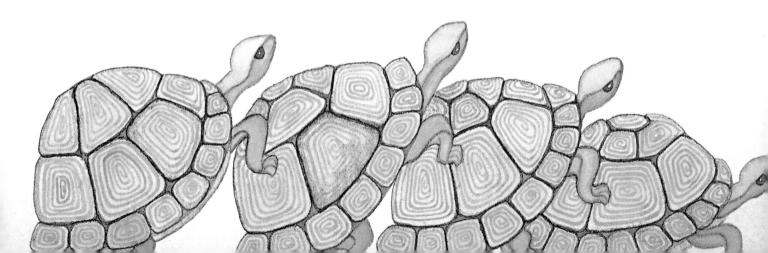

Change in the Air

Carbon dioxide in the air traps heat coming from the earth's surface. A greenhouse does the same thing. In a greenhouse, the sun's rays pass through the glass and warm up the soil and plants. The glass traps heat and makes the greenhouse warmer. As carbon dioxide is added to the earth's atmosphere, it creates a greenhouse effect. The earth gets warmer. The ice at the poles can melt, raising the level of the oceans. Coastal land would be lost and the world's rainfall patterns could change. No one knows for certain all that might happen, but we are starting to make changes to release as little carbon dioxide into the air as possible.

Destroying the rain forest will certainly change the climate of the region. Here's why: Great amounts of water evaporate into the air over the Atlantic Ocean. Rainy weather travels west over the Amazon basin. The forest absorbs rainwater like a sponge. But the trees return more than half of this rainwater back into the air. So the same water comes down again as rain, farther west. If large areas of rain forest are destroyed, rainwater will not be recycled. The heavy rains will not be absorbed by trees, producing heavy flooding. The minerals and other plant nutrients would be washed out of the soil. The area could become a desert. Scientists don't know how long this may take, but why wait until it's too late to prevent it?

🔹 A Fragile Balance 🔹

The scattered native Indian tribes of the rain forest know how to live in harmony with the jungle. They know its foods and its poisons. They know its medicines, some of which have helped the rest of the world. They create art from its plants and animals. There is a great deal to learn from them and from the rain forest itself. Scientists come here from all over the world to study the plants and animals and the ways they depend on each other. Here we can learn the balance between civilization and the wilderness. What can you do to help save the rain forest?